GOOD FOOD FOR
Diabetes

TARLA DALAL
India's # 1 Cookery Author

S&C
SANJAY & CO.
MUMBAI

Second Printing : 2006

Copyright © Sanjay & Co.

ISBN : 81-89491-14-8

RRP : £3.99

Published & Distributed by : **Sanjay & Company**

353/A-1, Shah & Nahar Industrial Estate, Dhanraj Mill Compound,
Lower Parel (W), Mumbai - 400 013. INDIA.
Tel. : (91-22) 2496 8068 ● Fax : (91-22) 2496 5876 ● E-mail : sanjay@tarladalal.com

Distributed in U.K. by : **Mr. Deepesh Chotai**

Gifts By Vishaldeep, 378 Romford Road, Forest Gate, London, E7 8BS
Tel : 0208 4700486 ● Website : www.vishaldeep.com ● Email : info@vishaldeep.com

Recipe Research & Production Design	**Nutritionists**	**Photography**	**Designed by**	**Copy Editor**
Arati Fedane	Nisha Katira	Jignesh Jhaveri	Satyamangal Rege	Ashvina Vakil
Umaima Abdually	Sapna Kamdar			
	Food Styling	**Typesetting**	**Printed by :**	
	Shubhangi Dhaimade	Adityas Enterprises	Minal Sales Agencies, Mumbai	

INTRODUCTION

The facts are alarming. According to World Health Organisation (WHO) surveys, 50 million people in India suffer from diabetes. Which means that one in every five Indians has diabetes, and since Indians are predisposed to the disease, that figure will continue to rise!

Diabetes (high blood sugar) is a lifelong condition that needs careful management in terms of diet, medication and exercise, of which diet is an top of the list. It's true that diabetics have to limit high-fat, high-sugar foods, but that doesn't mean they have to abstain from their favourite dishes. What's important is that they are careful about eating balanced meals, cooked healthily. In **Good Food For Diabetes**, my latest addition to the Total Health Series, I have compiled **44** diabetes-friendly recipes that can be easily worked into a daily diet.

Divided into carefully planned sections - **Soups, Salads, Stir-Fries, One-Dish Meals, In-Between-Meals, Main Course and Desserts,** these recipes are the result of painstaking research by my efficient team of chefs and nutritionists. We've taken diabetic-friendly ingredients and used them innovatively, such as **fenugreek (methi) seeds** in **Fruity Sprouts Salad, page 35; soya bean** in **Nutritious Burger, page 52; bitter gourd (karela)** in **Masala Karela, page 71; and fibre rich apples** in **Hot Apple Pie with Low Fat Custard, page 97.** While the salad and stir-fry recipes are loaded with nutrient and fibre-rich veggies, simple recipes for in-between-meals are ideal to help satiate the frequent hunger pangs diabetics face throughout the day. Popular desserts and accompaniments have been specially modified for diabetics, while the main course offers a selection of recipes from different cuisines that will add spice and variety to a routine diet.

The book also includes useful information such as **basic facts about diabetes, making the right food choice, nutrients that help to control diabetes and top 10 natural remedies for diabetes.**

If you're a diabetic or have one in the family, you will welcome this little book. I guarantee it will surprise you!

Happy cooking!

Regards

Tarla Dalal

CONTENTS

WHAT IS DIABETES?

Diabetes is a condition (disorder) that prevents the body from utilising glucose (sugar), thereby leading to a rise in blood glucose levels.

The food that we eat gets converted into simple sugar, i.e., glucose. Our body utilises glucose to produce energy required to perform various activities and bodily functions. Insulin, a hormone secreted by the beta cells of the pancreas, makes glucose available to the body cells, helping to convert it into usable energy. In case of lack of or insufficient insulin our body fails to utilise glucose to produce energy, thus increasing the levels of glucose in our blood and leading to the condition called Diabetes Mellitus.

TYPES AND CAUSES OF DIABETES

Diabetes is of different types, depending on factors such as cause, age of onset, treatment, etc.

TYPES	CAUSES	AGE OF ONSET	CHARACTERISTICS
1. Type I Diabetes Mellitus or Insulin Dependant Diabetes Mellitus (IDDM) or Juvenile Onset Diabetes	Heredity, inability of pancreas to produce insulin.	Usually a sudden onset and occurring in the younger age group.	Requires insulin injections to regulate blood glucose levels.
2. Type II Diabetes Mellitus or Non Insulin Dependant	Obesity, insulin insensitivity (excess deposition of fat on body cells makes them insensitive to insulin thereby	Develops slowly and is common in adults (35-40 years).	Does not require insulin injections but requires oral drugs to maintain blood glucose levels. Weight loss

... cont'd

TYPE	CAUSE	AGE OF ONSET	CHARACTERISTICS
Diabetes Mellitus (NIDDM) or Adult onset diabetes.	impairing glucose utilisation), heredity and other medical illnesses, infection, etc.		helps to improve the condition.
3. **Gestational Diabetes**	Pregnancy (because of the hormonal changes taking place during pregnancy).	Women of childbearing age (18-35 years).	Usually disappears post-delivery.

SYMPTOMS OF DIABETES

While the symptoms of diabetes may begin gradually and can be hard to identify at first, the classic symptoms are:

- POLYURIA - excessive urination
- POLYDIPSIA - excessive thirst
- POLYPHAGIA - increased hunger
- Weight loss (Type I) or obesity (Type II)

Other symptoms are fatigue, blurred vision, aches and pains, dry mouth, dry or itchy skin, vaginal yeast infections (in females) due to excretion of excess glucose in urine, poor healing of cuts and scrapes, excessive or unusual infections, and tingling or numbness in the hands or feet.

DEALING WITH DIABETES

A healthy diet, exercise and medication are essential to control and manage diabetes. Here are a few easy guidelines to help deal with diabetes more effectively.

9

Diet

✓ Maintain your weight at desirable levels. Type II diabetics if overweight and need to lose weight in order to control diabetes.

✓ Maintain regular meal timings and do not skip meals.

✓ Eat in a relaxed and stress-free environment as stress can impair the digestion of food and the production of insulin.

✓ Pick your food wisely. To make your food choices simpler and healthier just refer to the table **Make The Right Food Choice, page 11.**

✓ Do not eat large meals. Break up the total calories prescribed for a day into smaller meals at regular intervals (six to eight meals per day).

✓ Have an early dinner at least two to three hours before going to bed. Drink a cup of milk (low fat milk preferably) two hours after dinner to avoid hypoglycaemia during the night.

✓ Snacking during the day helps to handle frequent hunger pangs and prevent fluctuations in blood glucose levels. Remember however to choose the right kind of snacks. Refer to the section on **In-Between-Meals,** page 61, to simply your choice of snacks.

Medication

✓ Take your medication or insulin injection at the prescribed timings. Do not alter the dosage of insulin without consulting your diabetologist.

✓ Adjust the amount and timing of meals, dosage of medicine and level of physical activity to maintain normal blood glucose levels.

Exercise

✓ Try to maintain a moderate and regular exercise regime throughout the day. Regular exercise helps to regulate blood glucose levels, improve the action of insulin, lose weight, reduce stress, increase HDL (good cholesterol) and reduce LDL (bad cholesterol).

✓ Walk for at least 15 to 20 minutes after every meal. Brisk walking is the best form of exercise as it helps to improve digestion and the action of insulin on glucose.

✓ To remain fit and healthy make small changes in your daily routine: climb the stairs instead of taking the lift, walk small distances instead of taking a cab or take your pet for a walk.

✓ Exercising on an empty stomach may lead hypoglycaemia (low blood glucose levels), which may further lead to giddiness, headache, etc. Remember to eat something before embarking on any form of exercise.

✓ Before you start exercising consult a doctor about the type and duration of exercise best suited to you.

MAKE THE RIGHT FOOD CHOICE

Food Groups	Foods Allowed	Foods Not Allowed	Effect On Your Body
Cereals	Fibre-rich cereals (complex carbohydrates) like whole wheat flour (*gehun ka atta*), *bajra* (black millet), *ragi/ nachani* (red millet), *jowar* (white millet), wheat bran (*konda*), buckwheat (*kutti no daro*), rice bran, oats, barley, etc.	Simple carbohydrates like refined flour (*maida*) and its products like pasta, noodles, biscuits, bread, corn flour* and rice*.	Complex carbohydrates take longer to digest and are rich in fibre, leading to a more gradual rise in blood glucose levels as compared to simple carbohydrates. If you wish to eat rice or bread, try to pair it with lots of fibre-rich veggies to avoid a quick rise in blood glucose levels.

cont'd... 11

Food Groups	Foods Allowed	Foods Not Allowed	Effect On Your Body
	Bread, pasta and noodles made from whole wheat flour. Digestive and Marie biscuits.		
Pulses and Legumes	Red gram (*tur dal*), *chana dal* (Bengal gram), kidney beans (*rajma*), *Kabuli chana* (chick peas), whole green gram (*moong*), soya bean and its products, sprouts, red lentil (*masoor*) etc.	Canned beans.	Pulses are a rich source of protein, which is required in moderate quantities. Excess protein can cause an overload on the kidneys. Have only one source of protein in each meal or have small portions of any 2 sources. For example, do not combine pulses, *paneer* (cottage cheese), curds and milk in one meal.
Milk and Milk Products	Low fat milk and milk products like *paneer* (cottage cheese), cream*, curds (*dahi*), buttermilk, skim milk, milkshakes* and cheese*.	Full fat milk and milk products like *paneer* (cottage cheese), cream, curds (*dahi*), lassi, milkshakes, condensed milk and full fat ice	Milk and milk products are rich in protein and fat. It is advisable to opt for their low fat counterparts and include only one source of this food group in your daily diet.

cont'd... 12

Food Groups	Foods Allowed	Foods Not Allowed	Effect On Your Body
Vegetables	Fibre-rich vegetables like cabbage, cluster beans (*gavarfail*), french beans, onions, bitter gourd (*karela*) and all leafy vegetables like fenugreek (*methi*), spinach (*palak*), etc.	Carbohydrate-rich vegetables like potatoes*, yam*, beetroot* and sweet potatoes*.	Vegetables are rich in fibre, vitamins and minerals. Fibre helps to bind glucose and slow downs its absorption thereby preventing a sudden rise in blood glucose levels. Carbohydrate-rich veggies increase blood glucose levels rapidly therefore should be avoided or ocassionally be consumed in combination with other fibre rich foods.
Fruits	Fibre-rich and juicy fruits such as apple, watermelon, papaya, muskmelon, pineapple, orange, pears, guava etc.	Carbohydrate-rich fruits like chickoo*, mango*, banana*, custard apple*, grapes*, preserved or canned fruits, squashes and canned juices.	Choose juicy and fibre-rich fruits over carbohydrate-rich fruits because fructose, or fruit sugar, is also capable of a quick increase in blood glucose levels. It is advisable to eat one or two whole fruits in a day. Try to avoid juices as straining and other heat processes lead to loss of valuable nutrients, especially fibre and tend to raise blood sugar faster than whole fruits.

cont'd...

Food Groups	Foods Allowed	Foods Not Allowed	Effect On Your Body
Fats and Oils	Vegetable oils*, unrefined oil*, low fat butter*	Ghee, butter and mayonnaise.	Ghee, butter and mayonnaise are rich in saturated fats which tend to raise blood cholesterol levels which is a ladder to heart disease - a complication of diabetes. Restrict the amount of oil also to only 3 tsp per day to avoid unnecessary weight gain.
Nuts and Oilseeds	Walnuts*, almonds*and dates*.	Cashewnuts, pistachio nuts, coconut, poppy seeds (*khus-khus*), etc.	Nuts and oilseeds are rich in fat and protein and their consumption must be restricted. Walnuts and almonds contain MUFA (Mono Unsaturated Fatty Acids), beneficial fats that protect our heart. It is advisable to have these nuts 2-3 times a week provided you balance your energy intake on the day you have them. Dates can be used as a substitute to sugar to satisfy your sweet tooth ocassionally.
Miscellaneous	Artificial sweeteners*, tea*, coffee*, baked	Fried foods, farsan, wafers, pickles,	It is very important to restrict the amount of simple sugar as it

Food Groups	Foods Allowed	Foods Not Allowed	Effect On Your Body
	snacks/ farsans, spices like turmeric, garlic, fenugreek (*methi*) seeds, etc.	processed foods, papads, aerated drinks, alcohol, chocolates, full fat puddings, pies, desserts, cakes, candy, sugar, honey, jaggery, sweets like peda, barfi, high fat salad dressings etc.	drastically raises blood glucose levels. Do keep a check on sodium intake, as most diabetics are prone to high blood pressure. Try to restrict the use of other processed foods as these are high in salt, sugar, fat and preservatives and refined so devoid of any nutrient.

* These foods can be ocassionally consumed but in restricted amounts and in combination with other fibre rich foods preferably.

NUTRIENTS THAT HELP CONTROL DIABETES

✓ **Fibre** binds glucose, thus slowing its absorption and preventing a quick rise in blood glucose levels. It also helps to reduce blood cholesterol levels and avoid diabetes related complications like heart disease.

   Sources: Whole cereals, fresh fruits and vegetables, sprouts.

✓ **Vitamin C** is a potent antioxidant that protects our body against damage from free radicals, thus reducing the risk of developing degenerative diseases and diabetes-related complications. It also improves the action of insulin and helps to lower blood glucose levels. A sign of severe vitamin C deficiency, common to diabetics, is delay in wound healing.

   Sources: Citrus fruits like orange, sweet lime and pineapple and vegetables like cabbage, lettuce, capsicum, etc.

✓ **Potassium** improves insulin sensitivity and fosters optimum glucose utilisation. A potassium-rich diet also reduces the risk of heart disease and atherosclerosis.
Sources: Leafy vegetables like spinach, fenugreek. Fruits like banana, figs, citrus fruits and cereals like wheat, bajra, ragi etc.

✓ **Magnesium** plays a pivotal role in the secretion and function of insulin. Magnesium deficiency is common among diabetics and can lead to complications like heart disease, eye damage, high blood pressure, and obesity. Adequate magnesium intake improves the action of insulin, betters glucose tolerance and reduces the stickiness of red blood cell membranes.
Sources: Milk, cereals, soya bean, green vegetables and dry fruits.

✓ **B-complex vitamins** deficiency of B vitamins can lead to nerve damage in the hands and feet leading to numbness and tingling. Vitamin B6 deficiency has been linked to glucose intolerance, which is an abnormally high rise in blood glucose levels after eating. People with Type I diabetes develop antibodies that attack and destroy the insulin-producing cells in the pancreas; Niacin (vitamin B3) seems to help protect such cells from attack.
Sources: Cereals, vegetables, milk, pulses, yeast, egg, sprouts, etc.

✓ **Folic acid** is required to produce red blood cells and helps convert homocysteine (a harmful amino acid that causes heart diseases) into methionine, which protects the heart and reduces the risk of developing heart disorders, a long-term complication of diabetes.
Sources: Green leafy vegetables like spinach, pulses, tomatoes, carrots, etc.

✓ **Zinc** diabetics usually have low zinc levels since it is lost in urine and hence it is advisable to eat zinc rich foods necessary for maintaining the insulin producing cells.
Sources: Cereals, pulses and legumes, dry fruits, etc.

✓ **Iron** does not have a direct relation with the disease, but plays an important role in the production of red blood cells and maintaining normal blood flow. This avoids accumulation of glucose in one part of the body, which would otherwise lead to complications like cataract and kidney disorders. Maintaining normal blood circulation also ensures availability of nutrients and oxygen to each part of the body, especially the heart.

Sources: Cereals like wheat, ragi/*nachni*, pulses, soya bean, leafy vegetables like spinach, fenugreek and colcocasia.

TOP 10 NATURAL REMEDIES FOR DIABETES

They say "Your food shall be your medicine", and that is so true for diabetics. Mother nature has offered us a variety of foods that can actually work like medicines and help alleviate disease. Here are a few tried and tested home remedies to help control diabetes.

1. **Bitter Gourd (Karela):** Half a cup of bitter gourd (*karela*) juice with the seeds or one cup of the cooked vegetable should be consumed on an empty stomach or in between meals. To make it a part of your meal, try the Karela Stir-Fry, page 47 and Crispy Karela, page 66.
2. **Fenugreek (Methi):** Include at least half a cup of fenugreek (*methi*) leaves or sprouted seeds in your daily diet, or eat six to eight seeds (soaked in water overnight) on an empty stomach early in the morning with or without water. If you can't stomach *methi* by itself, try out the Methi Dal Dhokli, page 49, or Methi and Moong Stuffed Rotis, page 82.
3. **Onions:** Diabetics will benefit from eating at least one cup of raw or cooked onions everyday. Alternately, include onions in your cooking, try the Minty Couscous, page 34 and Stuffed Capsicum, page 68.
4. **Garlic:** Include one large clove of garlic in your daily diet. Garlic is also an important ingredient in recipes like Roasted Capsicum Soup, page 22 and Chilli Garlic Stir-Fry, page 45.

5. **Black Jamun:** Once or twice a day consume *black jamun* juice, or three to four pieces of the *jamun* fruit, or a teaspoonful of the dried mixture made from equal quantities of *jamun* powder, *amla* powder and *karela* powder. Though not heard commonly Black Jamun Ice-cream, page 89 makes a very interesting variation.

6. **Soyabean:** Diabetics can never have enough of soya beans in any form - whole beans, sprouts, soya milk or soya flour. For interesting soya recipes, check out Stir Fried Tofu, Mushrooms and Capsicum, page 43 and Nutritious Burger, page 52.

7. **Chana (Bengal Gram) Dal:** Eat at least half a cup of *chana dal* in the form of variations such as Panchkuti Dal, page 78, Diabetic Puranpoli, page 92.

8. **Low Fat Curds:** Include low fat curds and low fat buttermilk in your daily diet. Use it innovatively as in Tropical Salad, page 35 and Fatless Maa ki Dal, page 76.

9. **Fibre-rich Vegetables and Fruits:** Include green peas, cluster beans (*gavarfali*), leafy vegetables, and fruits like apple (with the skin) and guava in your daily diet to get fibre. Gavarfali ki Sukhi Subzi, page 73 is sure to hit the list.

10. **Cinnamon:** The bio-acitve compound in cinnamon has a potential to increase the activity of insulin in our body. Apart from using cinnamon in the tempering of your recipes try variations like Apple Cinnamon Soya Shake, page 64.

Granted diabetes is a tiresome condition to live with but it need not be a debilitating one. Exercise caution in what you eat and alter your lifestyle to include regular activity of some form, and you can lead a normal life provided you take your medication of course!

Diabetes Friendly Ingredient : **CHANA (BENGAL GRAM) DAL,**
Recipe : DIABETIC PURANPOLI, page 92 →

≈ *Soups* ≈

⊛ Moong Soup with Paneer ⊛

This old-fashioned soup is one many of us grew up on. Use low fat paneer and just 2 tsp of oil to make it diabetic-friendly.

Preparation time: 5 minutes.   Cooking time: 25 minutes.   Serves 4.

⅓ cup whole *moong* (whole green gram)
2 tbsp grated low fat *paneer* (cottage cheese), page 100
1 tsp cumin seeds *(jeera)*
½ tsp mustard seeds *(rai / sarson)*
¼ tsp asafoetida *(hing)*
½ tsp chopped green chillies
4-5 curry leaves *(kadi patta)*
1 tsp lemon juice
2 tsp oil
Salt to taste

For the garnish
2 tbsp chopped coriander

1. Wash and soak the moong for a few hours. Drain, add 3 cups of water and cook in a pressure cooker till the moong is cooked. Set aside.
2. Heat the oil in a non-stick pan and fry the cumin seeds and mustard seeds. When they crackle, add the asafoetida, green chillies and curry leaves and fry for a while.
3. Add the moong, lemon juice, paneer, salt and 1 cup of water and simmer for 4 to 5 minutes.
   Serve hot garnished with coriander.

Handy tip: To enhance the taste of the soup, add a pinch of sugar substitute just before serving.

Nutritive values per serving

Energy	Protein	Carbohydrates	Fat	Fibre
70 cal	3.4 gm	8.1 gm	2.7 gm	0.6 gm

❧ Roasted Capsicum Soup ❧

Bright red and flavourful, this soup is ideal for diabetics. Capsicum contains vitamin A, an antioxidant that helps to fight the free radicals that otherwise attack healthy cells and lead to complications.

Preparation time: 10 minutes.   Cooking time: 20 minutes.   Serves 4.

2 whole red capsicum
4 medium sized tomatoes
2 bay leaves (*tej patta*)
1 clove garlic
½ cup low fat milk, page 99
1 tbsp corn flour
Salt to taste

For the garnish
2 tbsp chopped coriander

1. Pierce the red capsicum with a fork and roast them over a flame till they turn black.
2. Cool, wash them and remove the skin, stem and seeds. Keep aside.

22

3. Cut the tomatoes into quarters and add approx. 3 cups of water, bay leaves and garlic and boil till the tomatoes are soft. Discard the bay leaves and keep aside.
4. Purée the capsicum and tomato mixture into a smooth paste.
5. Mix the corn flour and milk and add to the paste.
6. Add salt and simmer the soup for few minutes till it thickens. Serve hot garnished with coriander.

Handy tip: If the soup tastes sour add a pinch of sugar substitute and mix well just before serving.

Nutritive values per serving

Energy	Protein	Carbohydrates	Fat	Fibre	Vitamin A	Folic Acid
49 cal	2.6 gm	8.8 gm	0.5 gm	1.5 gm	670.3 mcg	23.4 mcg

⚜ Healthy Lentil Soup ⚜

This colourful soup makes an appealing entrée. Moong dal has a high potassium content which helps keep blood pressure under check.

Preparation time: 10 minutes.   Cooking time: 20 minutes.   Serves 4.

For the *moong dal* purée
3 tbsp yellow *moong dal* (split yellow gram)
½ cup chopped onions
¼ cup diced carrots

Other ingredients
½ cup chopped onions
½ tsp chopped garlic
2 tbsp chopped celery
2 tbsp cooked pearl barley (*jau*)
1 tbsp corn flour
2 tsp oil
Salt and freshly crushed pepper to taste

For the *moong dal* purée
1. Wash and soak moong dal for few hours.
2. Drain, add 3 cups of water, onions and carrots and pressure cook for 1 to 2 whistles.
3. When cooked, purée till smooth. Keep aside.

How to proceed
1. Heat the oil in non-stick pan and sauté the onions, garlic and celery for 1 minute.
2. Add the moong dal purée and bring to boil. Simmer for 3 to 4 minutes and stir in the cooked pearl barley, salt and pepper.
3. Mix the corn flour with ½ cup of water and add to the soup.
4. Simmer for another 3 to 4 minutes. Serve hot.

Handy tip: Pearl barley is easily available at local chemists. Wash it thoroughly and cook in boiling water like rice. The water in which barley is cooked is nutritious and rich in antioxidants that help to fight diseases. It can be used for kneading dough or added to buttermilk or soups.

Nutritive values per serving

Energy	Protein	Carbohydrates	Fat	Fibre	Potassium
81 cal	3.9 gm	15.6 gm	0.3 gm	0.7 gm	172.1 mg

❧ Mushroom Soup ❧

An easy-to-whip up and nourishing soup made from low calorie mushrooms and low fat milk.

Preparation time: 10 minutes.   Cooking time: 10 minutes.   Serves 4.

3 cups thickly sliced mushrooms
½ cup chopped onions
2 tsp plain flour (*maida*)

1 cup low fat milk , page 99
1 tsp oil
Salt and freshly crushed pepper to taste

1. Heat the oil in a non-stick pan, add the onions and sauté for 1 minute. Sprinkle a little water if the onions start burning.
2. Add the plain flour and mushrooms and fry for some more time.
3. Add milk and stir continuously till no lumps remain. Allow to cook.
4. When cooked, purée till smooth. Add 3 cups of water, salt and pepper.
5. Simmer for another 3 to 4 minutes. Serve hot.

Nutritive values per serving

Energy	Protein	Carbohydrates	Fat	Fibre	Potassium
65 cal	2.7 gm	8.0 gm	2.8 gm	0.7 gm	**201.5 mg**

❧ Vegetable Broth ❧

Provides an abundant supply of vitamin C, a powerful antioxidant that reduces the free-radical damage, which otherwise leads to heart disease, cancer, and other age-related degenerative diseases.

Preparation time: 15 minutes.   Cooking time: 10 minutes.   Serves 4.

2 tbsp finely chopped tomatoes
2 tbsp finely chopped capsicum
2 tbsp finely chopped cauliflower
2 tbsp finely chopped carrots
2 tbsp finely chopped cabbage
2 tsp finely chopped garlic
1 bay leaf (*tej patta*)
2 tbsp quick cooking rolled oats
1 tbsp fresh finely chopped mint (*phudina*) leaves
1 tbsp chopped coriander
2 tbsp finely chopped parsley
½ tsp marmite (optional)
2 tsp corn flour dissolved in ¼ cup water
2 tsp oil

Salt and freshly crushed pepper to taste

1. Heat the oil in a non-stick pan over a high flame. Add the garlic, bay leaf, vegetables and oats and stir-fry for 2 to 3 minutes.
2. Add 4 cups of water, mint, coriander, parsley, marmite, salt and pepper and bring to a boil.
3. Add the corn flour mixture to the soup and simmer for another minute.
4. Discard the bay leaf and serve hot.

Handy tip: Available at select stores, Marmite is a yeast extract rich in B-complex vitamins. It gives a distinctive flavour to the soup.

Nutritive values per serving

Energy	Protein	Carbohydrates	Fat	Fibre	Vitamin C
49 cal	1.2 gm	4.8 gm	2.9 gm	0.7 gm	29.3 mg

≈ Salads ≈

⚮ Mexican Salad ⚮

A simple potassium-rich Mexican concoction with a zingy salsa dressing….ideal to combat high blood pressure.

Preparation time: 15 minutes.   Cooking time: 5 minutes.   Serves 4.

1 cup boiled corn
1 cup chopped spring onions
½ cup chopped apples with the skin
1 cup boiled *rajma* (kidney beans)
1 cup low fat *paneer* (cottage cheese) cubes, page 100
¼ cup chopped coriander

For the salsa dressing

4 tomatoes
1 capsicum
1 onion, finely chopped
½ tsp chilli powder
¼ tsp oregano
1 tsp oil
Sugar substitute to taste
Salt to taste

For the salsa dressing
1. Put the tomatoes in a bowlful of hot water. After 10 minutes, remove, peel and discard the skin and chop them. Keep aside.
2. Pierce capsicum with a fork and roast it over a flame until the skin blackens.
3. Cool, wash and remove the skin, stem and seeds. Chop and keep aside.
4. Heat the oil in a non-stick pan and fry the onions for half a minute. Add the tomatoes, capsicum, chilli powder, oregano, sugar substitute and salt and cook for a few minutes. Keep aside.

How to proceed
Combine all the salad ingredients together in a bowl, add the salsa dressing and toss well.
Serve immediately.

Handy tip: To get 1 cup of boiled rajma, soak ⅓ cup of rajma in water overnight. Drain, wash, add water and salt and pressure cook till done.

Nutritive values per serving

Energy	Protein	Carbohydrates	Fat	Fibre	Potassium
182 cal	8.0 gm	32.5 gm	2.3 gm	3.2 gm	**284.0 mg**

❧ Cabbage and Pineapple Salad ❧

This healthier version of traditional coleslaw is full of powerful fighter vitamins A and C which block many of the deleterious effects of elevated glucose levels.

Preparation time: 10 minutes.   No cooking.   Serves 4.

1 cup shredded cabbage
½ cup pineapple cubes
1 cup coarsely grated carrots
½ cup shredded lettuce

2 tbsp pineapple juice or crushed pineapple
¼ cup chopped coriander
½ tsp black salt (*sanchal*)
Salt to taste

Combine all the ingredients together in a bowl and toss well.
Serve immediately.

Nutritive values per serving

Energy	Protein	Carbohydrates	Fat	Fibre	Vitamin A	Vitamin C
36 cal	1.2 gm	7.5 gm	0.2 gm	0.8 gm	**748.2 mcg**	**43.1 mg**

❧ Fruit and Vegetable Salad with Apple Dressing ❧

This innovative melange of fruit and vegetables is generously laced with iron, which maintains normal blood circulation, helping to improve nerve impulses that might otherwise deteriorate as diabetes progresses.

Preparation time: 10 minutes. No cooking. Serves 4.

½ cup cucumber cubes
½ cup chopped spring onions
½ cup papaya cubes
1 cup lettuce leaves, torn into pieces
½ cup capsicum cubes

¼ cup sliced avocado (optional)
Salt to taste

For the apple dressing (to be blended to a smooth purée)
¾ cup apple cubes, with the skin
1 tsp lemon juice

How to proceed
1. Combine all the salad ingredients together in a bowl.
2. Just before serving add the apple dressing and toss well. Serve immediately.

Nutritive values per serving

Energy	Protein	Carbohydrates	Fat	Fibre	Vitamin C	Iron
62 cal	1.6 gm	6.9 gm	3.2 gm	1.0 gm	40.3 mg	1.6 mg

❧ Mixed Sprouts Salad ❧

Maintain your blood sugar levels with this interesting combination of subtly spiced sprouts and vegetables.

Preparation time: 10 minutes.   Cooking time 2 minutes.   Serves 4.

¾ cup boiled mixed sprouts (*kabuli chana, moong, rajma, matki,* etc.)
¼ cup grated radish (*mooli*)
¼ cup chopped tomatoes
¼ cup chopped small fenugreek (*methi*) leaves
2 tbsp chopped coriander
Salt to taste

For the tempering
1 green chilli, slit
A pinch of asafoetida (*hing*)
1 tsp oil

1. Combine all the salad ingredients together in a bowl and keep aside.
2. Heat oil in a non-stick pan and add the green chillies and asafoetida.
3. Add all the other ingredients and toss well. Serve immediately.

Nutritive values per serving

Energy	Protein	Carbohydrates	Fat	Fibre	Iron
43 cal	1.9 gm	5.4 gm	1.5 gm	0.5 gm	0.6 mg

❧ Minty Couscous ❧

Traditionally eaten in North Africa, couscous is a great source of iron. Lemon juice in this variation provides vitamin C, which enhances the absorption of iron and improves blood circulation in diabetics.

Preparation time: 10 minutes.   Cooking time: 5 minutes.   Serves 4.

½ cup broken wheat (*dalia*)
½ cup low fat milk, page 99
½ cup chopped tomatoes
½ cup chopped spring onions
¼ cup chopped coriander

2 tbsp chopped mint (*phudina*)
2 tsp olive oil
2 tsp lemon juice
Salt to taste

1. Cook the broken wheat in ½ cup of milk for 10 minutes or till it is tender.
2. Drain and set aside to cool.
3. Add all the other ingredients and toss well.
4. Refrigerate for at least 1 hour before serving so that all the flavours blend. Serve chilled.

Nutritive values per serving

Energy	Protein	Carbohydrates	Fat	Fibre	Vitamin C	Iron
105 cal	2.6 gm	17.1 gm	2.9 gm	0.8 gm	**12.7 mg**	**1.6 mg**

✬ Tropical Salad ✬

Picture on page 37.

*Fenugreek does wonders to control blood sugar levels, and also provides fibre when sprouted.
Here it is imaginatively combined with fruit and vegetables to create an unusual salad.*

Preparation time: 15 minutes.   No cooking.   Serves 4.

¼ cup sprouted fenugreek (*methi*) seeds
½ cup apple cubes, with the skin
½ cup pomegranate (*anar dana*)
½ cup roughly chopped spinach (*palak*)
Salt to taste

For the fruity dressing
½ cup papaya cubes
¼ cup low fat thick curds (*dahi*), page 100

For the fruity dressing
1. Blend all the ingredients together in a liquidiser till smooth.
2. Refrigerate and use as required.

How to proceed

1. Combine all the salad ingredients together in a bowl.
2. Just before serving, add the dressing and toss well.
   Serve immediately.

Nutritive values per serving

Energy	Protein	Carbohydrates	Fat	Fibre	Folic Acid	Potassium
46 cal	2.0 gm	8.6 gm	0.4 gm	1.6 gm	13.8 mcg	86.5 mg

Diabetes Friendly Ingredient : **LOW FAT CURDS,**
Recipe : FRUITY SPROUTS SALAD, page 35 →

≈ Stir-fries ≈

◈ Indian Stir-fry ◈

Raw papaya, cabbage and capsicum combine in a delightful low calorie, low sodium, high vitamin A stir-fry to suit the Indian palate.

Preparation time: 5 minutes.   Cooking time: 7 minutes.   Serves 4.

1 cup thickly grated raw papaya
1 cup shredded cabbage
½ cup thinly sliced capsicum
½ tsp mustard seeds (*rai/ sarson*)
2 pinches asafoetida (*hing*)
1 green chilli, slit
¼ tsp turmeric powder (*haldi*)
½ tsp lemon juice
2 tsp oil
Salt to taste

For the garnish
2 tbsp chopped coriander

1. Heat the oil in a non-stick pan, and add the mustard seeds. When they crackle add the asafoetida and green chilli and sauté for a few seconds.
2. Add all the other ingredients and stir for about 2 to 3 minutes on a high flame. Serve hot garnished with coriander.

Nutritive values per serving

Energy	Protein	Carbohydrates	Fat	Fibre	Vitamin A	Sodium
47 cal	1.2 gm	5.5 gm	2.6 gm	0.5 gm	863.5 mcg	2.0 mg

⚜ French Beans Foogath ⚜

Perk up french beans with Indian spices in this interesting stir-fry. French beans contain fibre, which binds glucose and slows down its absorption, preventing a quick rise in blood sugar levels.

Preparation time: 5 minutes.   Cooking time: 15 minutes.   Serves 4.

3 cups french beans (*fansi*), stringed and thinly sliced
¼ cup *chana dal* (split bengal gram), soaked
½ tsp mustard seeds (*rai / sarson*)
1 tsp *urad dal* (split black lentils)
4-6 curry leaves (*kadi patta*)
¼ tsp asafoetida (*hing*)
1 tsp grated ginger
¼ tsp turmeric powder (*haldi*)
2 tsp oil
Salt to taste

For the garnish
¼ cup chopped coriander

1. Heat the oil in a non-stick pan and add the mustard seeds. When they crackle, add the urad dal and sauté for a few seconds.
2. Add the curry leaves, asafoetida and ginger and stir for a few more seconds.
3. Add the french beans, chana dal, turmeric powder, salt and ½ cup of water, mix well and cover with a lid.
4. Cook over a low flame till the french beans and chana dal are cooked.
5. Remove the lid, increase the flame and stir-fry over a high flame till all the water evaporates.
   Serve hot garnished with coriander.

Nutritive values per serving

Energy	Protein	Carbohydrates	Fat	Fibre	Zinc
84 cal	3.7 gm	10.2 gm	3.2 gm	1.5 gm	0.5 mg

✤ Broccoli Stir-Fry ✤

Potassium-rich and full of fibre, the broccoli in this delicately flavoured stir-fry helps improve insulin action and control blood sugar levels.

Preparation time: 5 minutes.   Cooking time: 10 minutes.   Serves 4.

1½ cups broccoli florets
½ cup thinly sliced broccoli stems
2 cups thickly sliced mushrooms
2 cups bean sprouts

3 cloves garlic, chopped
2 tsp thyme
2 tsp oil
Salt to taste

1. Boil some water in a large pan and blanch the broccoli florets, broccoli stems and mushrooms for ½ a minute. Drain and keep aside.
2. Heat oil in a non-stick pan and add the garlic and sauté for few seconds.
3. Add all the remaining ingredients and sauté for another 5 minutes. Serve hot.

Nutritive values per serving

Energy	Protein	Carbohydrates	Fat	Fibre	Potassium	Zinc
130 cal	8.1 gm	18.2 gm	3.0 gm	3.0 gm	444.2 mg	1.1 mg

❧ Stir-Fried Tofu, Mushrooms and Capsicum ❧

Picture on page 65.

A fibre-rich and fragrant variation of the Chinese classic that's brimming with Vitamin C!

Preparation time: 10 minutes.   Cooking time: 10 minutes.   Serves 4.

1 cup tofu (soya paneer) / low fat *paneer* (cottage cheese) cubes, page 100
1 cup sliced mushrooms
½ cup sliced coloured capsicum
1 cup cauliflower florets, parboiled
¼ cup chopped spring onion whites
1½ tsp grated garlic
1½ tsp soya sauce
2 tsp oil
Salt and freshly crushed pepper to taste

For the garnish
½ cup sliced spring onion greens

1. Heat the oil in a non-stick pan and add the spring onion whites and garlic and stir-fry over a high flame for a few seconds.
2. Add the capsicum, cauliflower and salt and stir-fry for 2 to 3 minutes.
3. Add the mushrooms, tofu/ paneer, soya sauce and pepper and stir-fry for a few more minutes on a high flame.
   Serve immediately garnished with spring onion greens.

Nutritive values per serving

Energy	Protein	Carbohydrates	Fat	Fibre	Vitamin C
50 cal	2.2 gm	4.6 gm	2.7 gm	1.0 gm	37.2 mg

❧ Chilli Garlic Stir-fry ❧

A creative way to have your daily quota of vegetables! Feel free to add veggies of your choice.

Preparation time: 20 minutes. Cooking time: 15 minutes. Serves 6.

½ cup cabbage, cut into cubes
½ cup spring onion whites, cut into quarters
1 cup spinach (*palak*), torn into pieces
¾ cup thickly sliced baby corn, parboiled
¾ cup broccoli florets parboiled
¾ cup snow peas, each cut into 2 and parboiled
½ cup capsicum, cut into cubes
½ cup sliced zucchini (optional)
1 tsp chilli-garlic paste
2 tsp corn flour mixed with ½ cup water
1 tbsp oil
Salt to taste

1. Heat the oil in a wok or a frying pan. Add the cabbage and ¼ cup water and allow to cook till the water evaporates and the cabbage is tender.
2. Add the spring onion whites and spinach and stir-fry for another minute.
3. Add all the other vegetables and the chilli-garlic paste and cook till the vegetables are tender but still crispy.
4. Add the corn flour paste and salt. Mix well and allow it to come to boil. Serve immediately.

Nutritive values per serving

Energy	Protein	Carbohydrates	Fat	Fibre	Vitamin A
56 cal	1.9 gm	6.9 gm	2.7 gm	1.1 gm	**891.4 mcg**

❧ Karela Stir-fry ❧

Picture on page 1.

Karelas are very diabetes-friendly, containing a high plant insulin dose that acts like human insulin in the body and help control blood sugar levels.

Preparation time: 5 minutes.   Cooking time: 20 minutes.   Serves 2.

1 cup peeled, deseeded and thinly sliced bitter gourd (*karela*)
1 cup finely chopped onions
A pinch of chilli powder
A pinch of turmeric powder (*haldi*)
A pinch of sugar substitute
1 tsp oil
Salt to taste

1. Apply a little salt to the bitter gourd slices and keep them aside for about 10 minutes.
2. Spoon the salted bitter gourd slices onto a kitchen towel and dab them lightly so that the towel absorbs all the moisture.

3. Spread the slices to form a thin layer in a microwave-safe dish and microwave on HIGH for 3 minutes, stirring once in between. Keep aside.
4. Meanwhile heat the oil in a non-stick pan add the onions and sauté till the onions turn golden brown.
5. Add all the remaining ingredients including the microwaved bitter gourd slices.
6. Allow to cook, stirring continuously till the slices become crisp.
   Serve hot.

Handy Tip: The microwave has been used to hasten the process. You can also make this dish on the gas; just remember to cook on a very low flame and stir continuously till the bitter gourd slices become crispy.

Nutritive values per serving

Energy	Protein	Carbohydrates	Fat	Fibre	Sodium	Potassium
68 cal	1.6 gm	9.5 gm	2.7 gm	0.8 gm	3.9 mg	171.0 mg

≈ One Dish Meals ≈

❧ Methi Dal Dhokli ❧

A Gujarati favourite, modified to include whole-wheat flour, minimum oil, sugar substitute, and fenugreek - just what the doctor ordered!

Preparation time: 20 minutes.   Cooking time: 40 minutes.   Serves 4.

For the dal
½ cup *toovar (arhar) dal*
¼ tsp mustard seeds (*rai / sarson*)
¼ tsp cumin seeds (*jeera*)
¼ tsp fenugreek (*methi*) seeds
5-6 curry leaves (*kadipatta*)
2 cloves (*laung/ lavang*)
2 sticks cinnamon (*dalchini*)
1 bay leaf (*tejpatta*)
2 small round red chillies (*boriya mirchi*)
¼ tsp asafoetida (*hing*)

4 pieces *cocum*, soaked
½ cup chopped tomatoes
½ tsp turmeric powder (*haldi*)
Juice of ½ lemon
4 green chillies, slit
½ tsp chilli powder
1 tsp grated ginger
1 tsp oil
1 tsp ghee
½ tsp (approx.) sugar substitute
Salt to taste

49

For the dhoklis
1 cup whole wheat flour (*gehun ka atta*)
¾ cup chopped fenugreek (*methi*) leaves
½ tsp turmeric powder (*haldi*)
½ tsp chilli powder
¼ tsp asafoetida (*hing*)
1 tsp oil
Salt to taste

For the garnish
¼ cup chopped coriander

For the dal
1. Wash and soak the dal for a few hours. Add 4 cups of water and cook in a pressure cooker. Keep aside to cool.
2. When the dal has cooled slightly, blend till it is smooth.
3. Heat the ghee and oil in a deep bottomed pan and add the mustard seeds, cumin seeds, fenugreek seeds, curry leaves, cloves, cinnamon, bay leaf, small round chillies and asafoetida and stir for 30 seconds.
4. Add 3 cups of water, cocum, tomatoes, turmeric powder, lemon juice, green chillies, chilli powder and ginger and simmer for 10 minutes.
5. Add the dal and salt and simmer for another 10 minutes.
   Keep aside.

For the dhoklis
1. Knead all the ingredients together with enough water to make firm dough.
2. Divide into four portions and roll out into thin chapattis.
3. Gently roast on both sides and cool.
4. Cut the chapattis into diamonds or squares and keep aside.

How to proceed
1. Just before serving boil the dal, add the dhokli pieces and simmer for 5 minutes. Add a little sugar substitute if necessary and mix well.
2. Garnish with coriander and serve hot.

Handy Tips: 1. Add the dhoklis into the dal one by one while stiring continuously to prevent lump formation.
2. Add more water if the dal thickens while simmering.

Nutritive values per serving

Energy	Protein	Carbohydrates	Fat	Fibre	Iron	Zinc
220 cal	9.1 gm	32.6 gm	5.9 gm	1.2 gm	2.2 mg	1.0 mg

❧ Nutritious Burger ❧

Picture on page 55.

Can't imagine healthy burgers? Try this brown bread-soya cutlet combination with low calorie Thousand Island dressing. The chemical choline in soya helps control diabetes and prevent nerve damage.

Preparation time: 20 minutes.   Cooking time: 5 minutes.   Makes 6.

For the burger
6 brown bread buns

For the cutlets
½ cup soya granules
¾ cup grated carrot
½ cup finely chopped onions
⅓ cup finely chopped mushrooms
¾ cup grated low fat *paneer* (cottage cheese), page 100
1 tsp soya sauce
1 tsp chilli sauce
2 tbsp whole wheat flour (*gehun ka atta*)
1½ tsp oil for cooking
Salt and freshly crushed pepper to taste

For the low calorie Thousand Island dressing
¼ cup thick fresh low fat curds (*dahi*), page 100
½ tsp mustard (*rai/ sarson*) powder
1½ tbsp tomato ketchup
½ tsp chilli sauce
1 tsp chopped onions
1 tsp chopped capsicum
¼ tsp chopped green chillies
A pinch sugar substitute
Salt to taste

Other ingredients
12 lettuce leaves
6 onion slices
12 cucumber slices
12 tomato slices

For the cutlets
1. Clean and wash the soya granules thoroughly and soak in 1 cup of hot water for 15 minutes. Drain the granules and discard the water.
2. Combine all the remaining ingredients in a bowl and mix well.
3. Divide the mixture into 6 equal parts and shape into flat patties.
4. Cook on a non-stick pan using a little oil till both sides are golden brown. Keep aside.

For the dressing
Mix all the ingredients thoroughly and keep aside.

How to proceed
1. Slice each bun into two halves and toast lightly in an oven or on a tava (griddle).
2. Spread some of the low calorie Thousand Island dressing on each half.

3. On one half, arrange 2 lettuce leaves, 1 cutlet, 1 onion slice, 2 cucumber slices and 2 tomato slices and cover with the other half of the bun.
Serve immediately.

Nutritive values per burger

Energy	Protein	Carbohydrates	Fat	Fibre	Iron	Zinc
231 cal	9.2 gm	40.0 gm	3.9 gm	**1.6 gm**	**3.7 mg**	**1.4 mg**

Diabetes Friendly Ingredient : **SOYA,**
Recipe : NUTRITIOUS BURGER, page 52 ➙

❧ Spicy Baked Dish ☙

Constant high blood sugar results in neuropathy or nerve damage, which hinders transmission of proper signals, resulting in a loss of sensation, hyper sensation or pain. Combat this risk by eating fibre-rich foods like mushrooms, which help maintain blood sugar levels.

Preparation time: 15 minutes.   Cooking time: 20 minutes.   Serves 4.
Baking time: 10 minutes.   Baking Temperature: 200°C (400°F).

6 half cooked whole wheat *chapattis*, page 102

For the mushroom filling
2 cups sliced mushrooms
¼ cup chopped onions
¼ tsp oregano
2 tbsp chopped coriander
1 tsp corn flour
2 tsp oil
Salt and freshly crushed pepper to taste

For the tomato sauce
2 cups chopped tomatoes
¼ cup chopped onions
2 cloves garlic
½ tsp chilli powder
Salt to taste

For the white sauce
1 tbsp whole wheat flour (*gehun ka atta*)
1 cup low fat milk, page 99
1 tsp oil
Salt and freshly crushed pepper to taste

For the mushroom filling
1. Heat the oil in a non-stick pan and sauté the onions till they turn translucent.
2. Add the mushrooms and sauté for a while.
3. Add the oregano, coriander, salt and pepper and mix well.
4. Sprinkle the corn flour over the mixture, mix well and cook for another 2 to 3 minutes. Divide into 6 equal portions and keep aside.

For the tomato sauce
1. Cook tomatoes, onions and garlic with ¾ cup of water till tomatoes are tender.
2. Remove the garlic and discard it. Cool completely.
3. Blend in a liquidiser till smooth using a little water.
4. Heat the purée in a non-stick pan and add chilli powder and salt and mix well. Keep aside.

For the white sauce
1. Heat oil in a non-stick pan and add the whole wheat flour and cook on a slow flame, stirring continuously, until froth appears.
2. Add the milk and ½ cup of water gradually and stir continuously until the sauce thickens.
3. Add salt and pepper and mix well. Keep aside.

How to proceed

1. Fill each *chapatti* with a portion of the mushroom filling and roll it up.
2. Arrange in a baking dish and pour the tomato sauce over the rolls.
3. Top with the white sauce and bake in a hot oven at 200°C (400°F) for 5 minutes. Serve hot.

Nutritive values per serving

Energy	Protein	Carbohydrates	Fat	Fibre	Vitamin C	Potassium
233 cal	8.3 gm	39.5 gm	4.9 gm	2.0 gm	26.6 mg	398.4 mg

❧ Double Decker Parathas ❧

A surprisingly low calorie version of the usually fattening paratha! Carrots abound in vitamin A, which nourishes the lining of the eyes, while the green peas add fibre and help to control blood sugar levels.

Preparation time: 20 minutes. Cooking time: 30 minutes. Makes 4.

12 whole wheat *chapattis*, page 102

For the carrot stuffing
½ cup grated carrots
1 tsp cumin seed (*jeera*)
½ tsp finely chopped green chillies
1 tsp lemon juice
½ tsp oil
Salt to taste

For the green peas stuffing
1½ cups boiled and mashed green peas

1 tsp cumin seeds (*jeera*)
1 tsp finely chopped green chillies
1 tbsp chopped coriander
½ tsp oil
Salt to taste

Other ingredients
2 tsp oil for cooking

59

For the carrot stuffing
1. Heat the oil in a non-stick pan and fry the cumin seeds until they crackle.
2. Add the carrots, green chillies, lemon juice and salt and mix well.
3. Cover and cook for 2 minutes. Keep aside.

For the green peas stuffing
1. Heat the oil in a non-stick pan and fry the cumin seeds until they crackle.
2. Add the green chillies, coriander and salt and cook for 1 minute.
3. Add the green peas and cook for another minute. Keep aside.

How to proceed
1. Spread 1 tbsp of the carrot stuffing on one chapatti and cover with another chapatti. Then spread 1 tbsp of the green peas stuffing, place another chapatti on the top and press firmly to seal the edges.
2. Cook the resultant double decker parathas on a tava (griddle) on both sides, using a little oil.
3. Repeat with the remaining chapattis and stuffing to make 3 more parathas. Serve hot.

Nutritive values per paratha

Energy	Protein	Carbohydrates	Fat	Fibre	Folic Acid
233 cal	9.3 gm	38.9 gm	4.5 gm	3.3 gm	21.5 mcg

≈ *In-Between-Meals* ≈
❧ Nutritious Thalipeeth ❧

A typical Maharashtrian snack, which can be whipped up in a jiffy and is an ideal choice to avoid fluctuations in blood sugar levels before lunch.

Preparation time: 4 minutes.　Cooking time: 10 minutes.　Makes 6.

3 tbsp *bajra* flour (black millet flour)
3 tbsp *jowar* flour (white millet flour)
3 tbsp whole wheat flour (*gehun ka atta*)
3 tbsp *besan* (bengal gram flour)
¾ cup shredded cabbage
¼ cup chopped onions
½ tsp finely chopped green chillies
½ tsp coriander-cumin seed (*dhania-jeera*) powder
2 tbsp chopped coriander
Salt to taste

Other ingredients
1 tsp oil for cooking

1. Mix all the ingredients together in a bowl and add enough water to make soft, loose dough. Divide it into 6 equal parts and set aside.
2. Heat a non-stick pan and grease it lightly with oil.
3. Spread a layer of the dough to form a pancake of 4 mm (⅛ ") thickness.
4. Cook on both sides till golden brown, using a little oil.
5. Repeat to make 3 more thalipeeth.
   Serve hot with chutney of your choice.

Nutritive values per *thalipeeth*

Energy	Protein	Carbohydrates	Fat	Fibre	Iron	Folic Acid	Sodium
70 cal	2.5 gm	11.9 gm	1.4 gm	0.4 gm	1.0 mg	12.7 mcg	5.3 mg

❧ Paneer Phudina Tikkis ❧

Use low fat paneer and minimal oil to cook these light and elegant tikkis, guaranteed to keep you going till lunch or dinner.

Preparation time: 5 minutes.   Cooking time: 5 minutes.   Makes 6 tikkis.

1 cup grated low fat *paneer* (cottage cheese), page 100
4 tbsp finely chopped mint (*phudina*)
½ tsp finely chopped green chillies
1 tbsp corn flour
Salt to taste

Other ingredients
2 tsp oil for cooking

For serving
1 tsp *chaat masala*

1. Combine all the ingredients in a bowl and mix well. Divide this mixture into 6 equal portions.
2. Shape each portion into a round and flatten slightly to make tikkis. Set aside.
3. Using a little oil, cook the tikkis on a non-stick pan till both sides are golden brown. Serve hot sprinkled with chaat masala.

Nutritive values per tikki

Energy	Protein	Carbohydrates	Fat	Fibre	Calcium	Sodium
27 cal	1.0 gm	1.9 gm	1.7 gm	0.2 gm	**36.0 mg**	**1.3 mg**

❧ Apple Cinnamon Soya Shake ❧

Picture on back cover.

A satiating fruity in-between snack…..that can be made in a jiffy. The antioxidents from soya, fibre from apples and the bio-active compound from cinnamon helps to avoid a quick rise in blood sugar levels and the low fat milk gives you enough calcium and protein while avoiding the unnecessary fat.

Preparation time: 10 minutes.   No cooking.   Serves 4.

3 apples, chopped
1 cup chilled soya milk
2 cups chilled low fat milk, page 99
½ tsp cinnamon (dalchini) powder

sugar substitute to taste

To Serve
ice-cubes

1. Blend the apple and sugar in a blender to a smooth purée using a little milk.
2. Add the cinnamon powder, soya milk and milk and blend again.
3. Pour into individual glasses and top with ice cubes. Serve immediately.

Nutritive values per serving

Energy	Protein	Carbohydrates	Fat	Fibre	Calcium
145 cal	5.5 gm	27.1 gm	1.7 gm	1.6 gm	**154.8 mg**

Diabetes Friendly Ingredient : **GARLIC,**
Recipe : STIR-FRIED PANEER, MUSHROOM AND CAPSICUM, page 43. ➜

⊰ Crispy Karela ⊱

Cook karela with flair to mask its bitter taste and benefit from its high potassium content, which helps to control blood sugar levels by increasing the action of insulin in the body.

Preparation time: 5 minutes.   Cooking time: 15 minutes.   Serves 2.

1 cup peeled, deseeded and thinly sliced bitter gourd (*karela*)
2 tsp *besan* (bengal gram flour)
A pinch of chilli powder
A pinch of turmeric powder (*haldi*)
½ tsp oil
Salt to taste

1. Apply a little salt to the bitter gourd slices and set aside for about 10 minutes.
2. Spoon the salted bitter gourd slices onto a kitchen towel and dab them lightly so that the towel absorbs all the moisture.
3. Remove onto a microwave safe dish and add all the remaining ingredients except the oil. Mix well.
4. Spread the slices to form a thin layer and microwave on HIGH for 3 minutes,

stirring once in between.

5. Heat the oil in a non-stick pan and add the microwaved bitter gourd slices. Keep stirring continuously till the slices become crisp.
   Cool and serve.

Handy Tip: The microwave has been used to hasten the process. You can also make this dish on the gas; just remember to cook on a very low flame and stir continuously till the karelas become crispy.

Nutritive values per serving

Energy	Protein	Carbohydrates	Fat	Fibre	Sodium	Potassium
35 cal	1.4 gm	3.4 gm	1.5 gm	0.4 gm	3.4 mg	108.8 mg

≈ *Main Course* ≈

⊷ Stuffed Capsicum ⊷

The generously spiced gravy combines with the vegetables and low fat paneer to provide a double dose of flavour, fibre and vitamin A. Serve hot with Kashmiri Rotis, page 80.

Preparation time: 30 minutes.   Cooking time: 15 minutes.   Serves 6.
Baking time: 5 minutes.   Baking temperature: 200°C (400°F).

8 medium sized capsicum

For the stuffing
1 cup chopped mixed boiled vegetables
(french beans, carrots, green peas)
½ cup crumbled low fat *paneer* (cottage cheese), page 100
½ tsp cumin seeds (*jeera*)
½ tsp chilli powder
½ tsp finely chopped green chillies
2 tbsp chopped coriander

1 tsp oil
Salt to taste

For the gravy
2 cups chopped tomatoes
½ cup sliced onions
¼ cup chopped red pumpkin (*kaddu*)
1 clove garlic, chopped
½ tsp grated ginger
1 stick cinnamon (*dalchini*)
2 cloves (*laung / lavang*)

½ tsp cumin seeds (*jeera*)
½ tsp chilli powder
½ tsp corn flour mixed in ½ cup low fat milk, page 99
2 tsp oil
Salt to taste

Other ingredients
½ tsp oil for greasing

1. Cut the tops of the capsicum and scoop out the centres.
2. Drop the shells in boiling water for a few minutes, drain and keep aside.

For the stuffing
1. Heat the oil in a non-stick pan and fry the cumin seeds for 1 minute.
2. Add all the remaining ingredients and cook for a few minutes. Keep aside.

For the gravy
1. Combine the tomatoes, onions, red pumpkin, garlic, ginger, cinnamon and cloves with ¾ cup of water and cook over a slow flame till the tomatoes and pumpkin are soft. Allow to cool completely, remove the cinnamon and cloves and discard them.
2. Blend the mixture into a smooth purée. Keep aside.

3. Heat oil in a non-stick pan and add the cumin seeds. When they crackle add the puréed tomato mixture, chilli powder and salt and simmer for 5 to 7 minutes.
4. Add the corn flour mixture and simmer for a couple of minutes again. Keep aside.

How to proceed
1. Stuff the capsicum with the stuffing.
2. Arrange them on a greased baking dish.
3. Pour the boiling gravy on top.
4. Bake in a hot oven at 200°C (400°F) for 10 minutes.
   Serve hot.

Nutritive values per serving

Energy	Protein	Carbohydrates	Fat	Fibre	Vitamin A
134 cal	5.7 gm	18.0 gm	4.6 gm	3.5 gm	1480.0 mcg

❧ Masala Karela ❧

A sweet and spicy way to make karelas more palatable and keep a check on blood sugar as well!
Serve with hot phulkas.

Preparation time: 10 minutes.   Cooking time: 20 minutes.   Serves 2.

1 cup peeled, deseeded and thinly sliced bitter gourd (*karela*)
1 cup finely chopped onions
½ cup chopped tomatoes
A pinch of chilli powder
A pinch of coriander-cumin seed (*dhania-jeera*) powder
A pinch of turmeric powder (*haldi*)
A pinch sugar substitute
2 tsp oil
Salt to taste

1. Apply a little salt to the bitter gourd slices and keep aside for about 10 minutes.
2. Spoon the salted bitter gourd slices onto a kitchen towel and dab them lightly so that the towel absorbs all the moisture.

3. Heat the oil in a non-stick pan and add the bitter gourd slices. Cook stirring continuously for about 10 minutes or till the slices turn golden brown.
4. Add the onions and fry again for a few more minutes.
5. Add the tomatoes, chilli powder, coriander-cumin seed powder, turmeric powder, sugar substitute and salt and fry again for some more time.
   Serve hot.

Nutritive values per serving

Energy	Protein	Carbohydrates	Fat	Fibre	Vitamin C	Potassium
49 cal	1.0 gm	5.4 gm	2.6 gm	0.6 gm	31.3 mg	114.0 mg

❧ Gavarfali ki Sukhi Subzi ❧

Picture on page 75.

The benefits of fibre-rich cluster beans are enhanced by the introduction of flavour-imparting garlic, which also keeps a check on blood sugar and cholesterol levels.

Preparation time: 10 minutes.   Cooking time: 15 minutes.   Serves 4.

2 cups cluster beans (*gavarfali*) cut into 25 mm. (1") pieces
A pinch of soda bi-carb (optional)
½ tsp cumin seeds (*jeera*)
2 tsp ginger-green chilli paste
4 cloves garlic, crushed
½ cup chopped onions
¼ tsp turmeric powder (*haldi*)
2 tsp coriander-cumin seed (*dhania-jeera*) powder
½ tsp chilli powder
2 tsp oil
Salt to taste

1. Heat the oil in a pressure cooker and add the cumin seeds.
2. When the seeds crackle, add the ginger-green chilli paste and garlic and sauté for a few seconds.
3. Add the onions and sauté till they turn translucent.
4. Add the cluster beans and 3 to 4 tbsp of water and pressure cook for 1 whistle. Cool completely.
5. Open the lid of the pressure cooker and add the turmeric powder, coriander-cumin seed powder, chilli powder and salt and cook for the another 3 to 4 minutes or till all the water evaporates.

   Serve hot.

Nutritive values per serving

Energy	Protein	Carbohydrates	Fat	Fibre	Folic Acid	Sodium
39 cal	1.8 gm	7.2 gm	2.7 gm	1.7 gm	73.0 mcg	0.7 mg

Diabetes Friendly Ingredient : **GAVARFALI,**
Recipe : GAVARFALI KI SUKHI SUBZI, page 73. →

❧ Fatless Maa ki Dal ❧

A healthier version of the traditional North Indian staple. Brimming with potassium, vitamin C and zinc it uses low fat curds for texture and eliminates oil/ghee completely.

Preparation time: 15 minutes.   Cooking time: 20 minutes.   Serves 4.

For the dal
¾ cup *chilkewali urad dal* (split black lentils)
1 cup grated onions
1 cup grated tomatoes
½ tsp turmeric powder (*haldi*)
2 tsp coriander-cumin seed (*dhania-jeera*) powder
1 tsp chilli powder
¾ cup low fat curds (*dahi*), beaten, page 100
Salt to taste

To be ground into a paste
50 mm. (2") piece ginger
2 green chillies

2 to 3 cloves garlic

For the garnish
2 tbsp chopped coriander

1. Clean, wash and soak the urad dal for 2 to 3 hours. Drain and set aside.
2. Mix the urad dal and onions with 1½ cups of water and cook in a pressure cooker until soft. Mash slightly.
3. Add the tomatoes, turmeric powder, ground paste, coriander-cumin seed powder, chilli powder and salt. Cook for 5 to 7 minutes or until the dal thickens.
4. Add the curds and mix well.
   Serve hot garnished with coriander.

Nutritive values per serving

Energy	Protein	Carbohydrates	Fat	Fibre	Potassium	Vitamin C	Zinc
140 cal	8.7 gm	25.1 gm	0.6 gm	0.9 gm	**343.9 mg**	**17.9 mg**	**1.0 mg**

❧ Panchkuti Dal ❧

This appealing combination of five dals and a blend of Indian spices is low in sodium and provides adequate protein, calcium and folic acid.

Preparation time: 15 minutes.   Cooking time: 25 minutes.   Serves 6.

1 tbsp chilkewali *urad dal* (split black lentils)
1 tbsp *toovar (arhar) dal*
1 tbsp green *moong dal* (split green gram)
1 tbsp *chana dal* (split bengal gram)
1 tbsp *masoor dal* (split red lentils)
1 tsp mustard seeds (*rai/sarson*)
1 tsp cumin seeds (*jeera*)
12 mm (½") stick cinnamon (*dalchini*)
2 cloves (*laung/lavang*)
4 curry leaves (*kadi patta*)
4 small whole dry red chillies
3 green chillies, finely chopped
2 tsp finely chopped ginger

2 tsp finely chopped garlic
2 tomatoes, roughly chopped
½ tsp *garam masala*
2 tbsp chopped coriander
1 tbsp lemon juice
1 tbsp oil
Salt to taste

1. Wash all the dals. Soak for 1 hour and then drain.
2. Add 3½ cups of water and cook in a pressure cooker until soft.
3. Heat the oil in a non-stick pan and fry the mustard seeds, cumin seeds, cinnamon and cloves.
4. When they begin to crackle, add the curry leaves, red chillies, ginger and garlic and fry for 1 minute.
5. Add the tomatoes, garam masala, dals, coriander, lemon juice and salt and boil for 8 to 10 minutes.
   Serve hot.

Nutritive values per serving

Energy	Protein	Carbohydrates	Fat	Fibre	Calcium	Folic Acid
70 cal	3.0 gm	8.2 gm	2.8 gm	0.6 gm	25.7 mg	21.0 mcg

❧ Kashmiri Rotis ❧

Indian spices add an exotic touch to whole wheat rotis, made with minimal oil. Ideal for diabetics who want to add flavour to a routine diet.

Preparation time: 10 minutes.   Cooking time: 20 minutes.   Makes 6 rotis.

1½ cups whole wheat flour (*gehun ka atta*)
½ tsp fennel seeds (*saunf*)
½ tsp cumin seeds (*jeera*)
¼ tsp *ajwain* (carom seeds)
8 to10 peppercorns
A pinch asafoetida (*hing*)
½ cup low fat milk, page 99
Salt to taste

Other ingredients
Whole wheat flour (*gehun ka atta*) for rolling
1½ tsp oil for cooking

1. Lightly roast the fennel seeds, cumin seeds, ajwain and peppercorns on a tava

(griddle). Coarsely pound the roasted ingredients in a mortar and pestle. Keep aside.
2. Combine the wheat flour, pounded masala, asafoetida, milk and salt and add enough water to make firm dough. Knead well.
3. Divide the dough into 6 equal portions.
4. Roll out each portion into a circle of 150 mm (6") diameter using a little whole wheat flour.
5. Using a little oil, cook each roti on a non-stick pan until both sides are golden brown.
   Serve hot.

Nutritive values per *roti*

Energy	Protein	Carbohydrates	Fat	Fibre	Iron	Sodium
108 cal	3.7 gm	19.5 gm	1.7 gm	0.5 gm	1.4 mg	5.4 mg

❧ Methi and Moong Stuffed Rotis ❧

Picture on page 85.

Fibre-rich moong sprouts and fenugreek are the twin pillars of these diabetic-friendly rotis, served with low fat curds.

Preparation time: 10 minutes.   Cooking time: 20 minutes.   Makes 6 rotis.

6 whole wheat *chapattis*, page 102

For the stuffing
¾ cup sprouted whole *moong* (whole green gram)
¾ cup finely chopped small fenugreek (*methi*) leaves
1 tsp finely chopped green chillies
1½ tsp *amchur* (dry mango powder)
¼ cup finely chopped coriander
A pinch turmeric powder (*haldi*)
Salt to taste

Other ingredients
Whole wheat flour (*gehun ka atta*) for rolling
2 tsp oil for cooking

For the stuffing
1. Boil the moong sprouts in very little water and a pinch of turmeric powder. Do not overcook. Drain and set aside.
2. Combine all the ingredients in a bowl and mix well.
3. Divide into 6 equal portions and keep aside.

How to proceed
1. Brush both sides of a *chapatti* with a little oil and place on a hot tava (griddle).
2. Put 1 portion of the stuffing on one half of the *chapatti*.
3. Fold the *chapatti* into a semi-circular shape keeping the stuffing in the centre.
4. Cook on both sides using oil till brown spots appear on the surface.
5. Repeat with the remaining *chapattis* and stuffing to make 5 more rotis.
   Serve hot.

Handy tip: The rotis can be stored in air-tight containers in the freezer for up to 2 months. Just defrost before use.

Nutritive values per *roti*

Energy	Protein	Carbohydrates	Fat	Fibre	Iron	Zinc
131 cal	5.1 gm	22.8 gm	2.2 gm	0.8 gm	1.7 mg	0.8 mg

❧ Wholesome Pulao ❧

Picture on cover.

Rice is usually a no-no for diabetics because it causes a quick rise in blood sugar levels. To counter the effect of rice, toss in some fibre-rich vegetables and other diabetic-friendly ingredients like garlic and fenugreek to create a hearty pulao.

Preparation time: 20 minutes.   Cooking time: 30 minutes.   Serves 4.

1 cup fat grained rice
1 green chilli, deseeded and sliced
25 mm (1") piece ginger, chopped
1 tbsp chopped garlic
1 cup finely chopped onions
½ cup finely chopped tomatoes
2 cups finely chopped fenugreek (*methi*) leaves
2 small brinjals, cut into big pieces

Diabetes Friendly Ingredient : **FENUGREEK (METHI)**,
Recipe : METHI AND MOONG STUFFED ROTIS, page 82. ➜

½ cup fresh double beans (*pavta*), boiled or soaked and cooked dried double beans
4 mushrooms, cut into thick slices
1 tsp chilli powder
2 tsp oil
Salt to taste

For the garnish
2 tbsp chopped coriander

1. Heat the oil in a pressure cooker, add the green chilli slices, ginger, garlic and onions and sauté till the onions turn translucent.
2. Add the tomatoes, fenugreek leaves, brinjals, cooked double beans, mushrooms and chilli powder, mix well and cook for a few minutes.
3. Add the rice and 2½ cups of hot water and salt and pressure cook for 3 whistles. Serve hot garnished with coriander.

Nutritive values per serving

Energy	Protein	Carbohydrates	Fat	Fibre	Vitamin A	Iron
226 cal	**6.6 gm**	43.0 gm	3.1 gm	**1.1 gm**	635.7 mcg	**1.3 mg**

Gehun ki Bikaneri Khichdi

This fibre and iron-rich whole wheat khichdi uses equal amounts of ghee and oil to give it that traditional touch, but you should avoid the ghee completely if you have high cholesterol along with diabetes.

Preparation time: 15 minutes. Cooking time: 15 minutes. Serves 4.

1 cup whole wheat (*gehun*)
¼ cup yellow *moong dal* (split yellow gram)
¼ tsp cumin seeds (*jeera*)
2 green chillies, slit
¼ tsp asafoetida (*hing*)
¼ tsp turmeric powder (*haldi*)
1 tsp oil
1 tsp ghee
Salt to taste

1. Clean, wash and soak the wheat overnight. Drain and set aside.
2. Clean, wash and soak the moong dal for 2 to 3 hours. Drain and set aside.
3. Grind the wheat to a coarse paste in a blender without using any water.

87

4. Heat the oil and ghee in a pressure cooker and add the cumin seeds, green chillies and asafoetida.
5. When the seeds crackle, add the ground wheat and moong dal and sauté for 4 to 5 minutes.
6. Add the turmeric powder, salt and 3½ cups of hot water and pressure cook for 6 to 7 whistles or until the wheat is cooked.

Serve hot.

Nutritive values per serving

Energy	Protein	Carbohydrates	Fat	Fibre	Iron
165 cal	6.3 gm	27.7 gm	3.2 gm	1.0 gm	1.4 mg

≈ Desserts ≈

The sweetness of sugar substitutes available in the market vary so please adjust the proportions according to the brand you use. Also confirm whether the sugar substitute can withstand the high temperatures of cooking. If not, make sure you add it after you switch off the flame.

❧ Black Jamun Ice-cream ❧

Picture on page 2.

The enzyme 'jamboline' in black jamuns is considered to be a boon for diabetics. So this rich, creamy, ice-cream made with reduced milk, thickened with cornflour and sweetened with sugar substitute is for all those who don't like to eat the fruit raw yet want to benefit from it.

Preparation time: 20 minutes.   Cooking time: 10 minutes.   Serves 4.

2½ cups (½ litre) low fat milk, page 99
2 tbsp cornflour
1½ cups chopped fresh black jamun
4 tsp (approx.) sugar substitute

1. Mix the cornflour in ½ cup of cold milk and keep aside.
2. Bring the remaining milk to a boil in a non-stick pan and add the cornflour

89

mixture.

3. Stir continuously and simmer over a slow flame till it coats the back of a spoon.
4. Cool completely. Add the sugar substitute and the black jamun. Mix well and pour into an air-tight container.
5. Freeze for 4 to 6 hours.
6. Liquidise in a blender till it is slushy and pour back into the air-tight container.
7. Freeze till the ice-cream is set.

Handy tip : Taste the ice-cream mixture after you add and mix each sachet to ascertain how much you need to add.

Nutritive values per serving

Energy	Protein	Carbohydrates	Fat	Fibre	Vitamin C	Calcium
101 cal	5.6 gm	18.7 gm	0.3 gm	0.3 gm	14.6 mg	183.2 mg

❦ Paneer Kheer ❦

Satisfy your sweet tooth with this cardamom-flavoured low fat paneer kheer, made with sugar substitute in replacement to sugar.

Preparation time: 5 minutes.   Cooking time: 15 minutes.   Serves 4.

3 cups low fat milk, page 99
1¼ cups grated low fat *paneer* (cottage cheese), page 100
2 tsp corn flour mixed with 1 tbsp low fat milk, page 99

A pinch of cardamom (*elaichi*) powder
3 tsp (approx.) sugar substitute

1. Mix together the milk and paneer in a broad non-stick pan and simmer on a flame, stirring continuously, for about 10 minutes. Add the corn flour mixture and stir continuously till it thickens.
2. Add the cardamom powder and sugar substitute and mix well. Serve chilled.

Nutritive values per serving

Energy	Protein	Carbohydrates	Fat	Fibre	Sodium
64 cal	5.4 gm	10.3 gm	0.2 gm	0 gm	1.3 mg

❧ Diabetic Puranpoli ❧

Picture on page 19.

An ocassional Sunday lunch, made diabetic-friendly by using sugar substitute and minimal ghee.

Preparation time: 10 minutes.   Cooking time: 10 minutes.   Makes 8 puranpolis.

For the dough
1½ cups whole wheat flour (*gehun ka atta*)
4 tbsp low fat milk, page 99

For serving
1½ tsp ghee for cooking

For the filling
1 cup *chana* (split Bengal gram) *dal*
3 tsp (approx.) sugar substitute

Other ingredients
Whole wheat flour (*gehun ka atta*) for rolling

For the dough
1. Make soft dough using the flour, milk and a little water (if required). Knead it well.
2. Divide the dough into 8 equal portions and set aside.

For the filling
1. Clean, wash and soak chana dal for 1 hour.
2. Drain the soaked chana dal, add ½ cup of water and cook it in a pressure cooker for 2 to 3 whistles.
3. Lightly mash the dal, add the sugar substitute and mix well. Cool completely and keep aside.

How to proceed
1. Roll out one portion of the dough into a circle of 75 mm (3") diameter using a little flour.
2. Place a portion of the filling in the centre of the circle.
3. Bring together all the sides in the centre and seal tightly.
4. Roll out again into a circle of 75 mm (3") diameter using a little flour.
5. Cook on a non-stick pan until both sides are brown.
6. Repeat with the remaining dough and filling to make 7 more puranpolis.

Nutritive values per *puranpoli*

Energy	Protein	Carbohydrates	Fat	Fibre	Calcium	Potassium	Zinc
198 cal	9.6 gm	34.9 gm	2.2 gm	0.9 gm	57.7 mg	386.8 mg	0.8 mg

❧ Rose Sandesh ☙

This delicately flavoured and fragrant sandesh is a healthy way to end your meal without adding any unnecessary calories and fat.

Preparation time: 30 minutes.   Cooking time: 10 minutes.   Makes 10 pieces.

2 litres low fat milk, page 99
½ tsp citric acid (*nimbu ka sar*)
2 tsp (approx.) sugar substitute
A few drops of rose essence
A few crushed rose petals

For the garnish
A few rose petals

1. Heat the milk in a vessel. When it starts boiling add citric acid. Stir continuously using a wooden spoon till it curdles completely. Remove from flame.
2. Drain the curdled milk through a fine muslin cloth and wring it to squeeze out excess water from the resultant paneer.

3. Open the cloth and mash the paneer with your palm on the cloth itself. If the paneer is hot use the edge of the cloth to rub it.
4. Remove the paneer onto the kitchen platform and rub in the sugar substitute according to taste. Add the rose essence and crushed rose petals.
5. Knead well to bind and get rid of any lumps.
6. Make 10 small round portions of the paneer, big enough to fit in the sandesh/ moulds.
7. Press the rounds on the sandesh moulds and shape accordingly.
8. Garnish with rose petals, unmould and store refrigerated.
   Serve chilled.

Handy tip: If sandesh moulds are not available you can use plastic or rubber chocolate moulds or simply shape the sandesh into small rounds or any other interesting shape.

Nutritive values per piece

Energy	Protein	Carbohydrates	Fat	Fibre	Iron
58 cal	**5.0 gm**	9.2 gm	0.2 gm	0 gm	**0.4 mg**

❧ Fruit Mould ❧

A sweet way to add fibre-laden fruits to your diet. The vitamin A from oranges helps to eliminate the harmful free radicals from the body and prevent other diseases like cancer and heart attacks.

Preparation time: 5 minutes.   Cooking time: 10 minutes.   Serves 2.

1 cup fresh orange juice
3 gms agar-agar
1 tsp lemon juice
¼ cup chopped fresh fruits (apple with the skin, guava, pear, orange, etc.)
1 tsp (approx.) sugar substitute

1. Heat the juice in a non-stick pan, add agar-agar and stir continuously till it melts.
2. Add the lemon juice, chopped fruits and sugar substitute and mix well.
3. Remove from the fire and cool completely.
4. Pour it into a jelly mould.
5. Refrigerate till set. Serve chilled.

Nutritive values per serving

Energy	Protein	Carbohydrates	Fat	Fibre	Vitamin A
94 cal	1.3 gm	21.8 gm	0.5 gm	1.0 gm	1944.4 mcg

❧ Hot Apple Pie with Low Fat Custard ❧

Devoid of sugar and cream, this finger-licking dessert offers the benefits of apples, wheat bran, oats, sugar substitute and low fat milk.

Preparation time: 15 minutes.   Cooking time: 15 minutes.   Serves 4.
Baking time: 20 minutes.   Baking temperature: 200°C (400°F).

For the low fat custard
1 cup low fat milk, page 99
2 tsp custard powder
1 tsp (approx.) sugar substitute
A few drops of vanilla essence

For the hot apple pie
2 cups sliced apple with the skin
¼ cup wheat bran (*konda*)
2 tbsp skim milk powder
2 tbsp choco protein powder
½ tsp vanilla essence
1 tsp (approx.) sugar substitute
¼ tsp oil for greasing

For the topping

½ cup quick cooking rolled oats

For the low fat custard

1. Mix the custard powder in ¼ cup milk and keep aside.
2. Heat the remaining milk with the sugar substitute in a non-stick saucepan.
3. When the milk starts boiling, add the custard powder mixture and vanilla essence.
4. Cook over a low flame, stirring continuously till the mixture thickens.
5. Pour into a bowl and keep aside to cool and then refrigerate to chill.

For the hot apple pie

1. Mix all the ingredients together in a bowl.
2. Put the mixture in a greased baking dish and sprinkle the oats on top and bake at
   200°C (400°F) for about 15 minutes.
   Serve hot with low fat custard.

Handy tip : Choco protein powders are available under various brandnames like
Complan, Boost, Proteinules etc.

Nutritive values per serving

Energy	Protein	Carbohydrates	Fat	Fibre	Iron	Zinc
140 cal	6.4 gm	24.5 gm	1.8 gm	1.7 gm	2.3 mg	0.9 mg

≈ Basic Recipes ≈
❧ Low Fat Milk ❧

Made from skimmed milk powder available at all leading grocery stores, low fat milk is virtually fat free but has the all the goodness of milk including protein, calcium and vitamin B2. Use low fat milk in gravies or desserts or to make other diary products like curds and paneer. Which amounts to only 71 calories per cup in comparison to 234 calories and 13 grams of fat per cup of full fat milk. Alternatively, you can use 99% fat free milk (low fat milk) available in tetra packs.

Preparation time: 5 minutes.   Cooking time: 7 minutes.   Makes 1 litre (5 cups).

100 grams skim milk powder   1 litre water

1. Mix the skim milk powder in 1½ cups of water and make a smooth paste.
2. Add the remaining water and if desired, mix with a whisk.
3. Boil and use as required.

Nutritive values per cup

Energy	Protein	Carbohydrates	Fat	Fibre
71 cal	7.6 gm	10.2 gm	0 gm	0 gm

❧ Low Fat Curds ❧

Curds are a wholesome and nourishing addition to your diet. Easier to digest than milk, curds complement the protein present in cereals like parathas and biryanis. Use this low fat version of curds as an accompaniment to the main meal or in raitas and salad dressings.

Preparation time: 5 minutes.   Cooking time: 6 hours.   Makes 5 cups.

1 litre low fat milk, page 99   1 tbsp curds (*dahi*)

1. Warm the milk.
2. Add the curds and mix well.
3. Cover and keep aside till the curds set (approximately five to six hours). During the cold season, place inside a cupboard or closed oven to set.

Nutritive values per cup

Energy	Protein	Carbohydrates	Fat	Fibre
75 cal	7.7 gm	10.4 gm	0.2 gm	0 gm

❧ Low Fat Paneer ❧

Prepared from low fat milk, low fat paneer has all the goodness of milk without its fat content. This is a superb way of adding protein (necessary for maintenance of body cells) and calcium (necessary for healthy bones) to a diabetic diet. Use it to make interesting snacks, subzis, and desserts.

Preparation time: 10 minutes.   Cooking time: 10 minutes.   Makes 100 grams
(approx. ¾ cup).

2 cups low fat milk, page 99
1 cup low fat curds (*dahi*), beaten, page 100

1. Put the milk to boil in a saucepan. When it starts boiling, add the low fat curds and mix well.
2. Remove from the heat and stir gently until the milk curdles.
3. Strain the curdled milk through a muslin cloth, bring the edges of the cloth together, tie and hang for about half an hour to allow the whey to drain out. Use as required.

Handy tips: 1. If the milk has not curdled completely in step 2, heat the mixture for a little more time.
2. Don't discard the whey, which is very nutritious. Use it to replace water while kneading dough, or add it to juices or buttermilk.

Nutritive values for 100 grams (¾ cup)

Energy	Protein	Carbohydrates	Fat	Fibre
232 cal	23.4 gm	31.4 gm	0.1 gm	0 gm

⋇ Whole Wheat Chapattis ⋇

High fibre, nuttri-loaded chapattis.... a perfect substitute to those made with maida.

Preparation time: 10 minutes.   Cooking time: 15 minutes.   Makes 6 chapattis.

1 cup whole wheat flour (*gehun ka atta*)   1 tsp oil
½ tsp salt   whole wheat flour (*gehun ka atta*) for rolling

1. Combine the flour and salt and knead into a soft and pliable dough.
2. Add the oil and knead again till it is smooth and elastic. Cover and keep aside for 10 to 15 minutes.
3. Divide the dough into 6 equal parts. Roll out each one using a little flour into approx. 150 mm. (6") diameter circles. Dust dry flour as required to facilitate even rolling.
4. Dust off any excess dry flour and place the chapatti on a hot tava.
5. Turn over in a few seconds and cook this side till the edges begin to curl slightly and small blisters appear on the surface. Cook the other side for a few more seconds.
6. Repeat to make 5 more half cooked chapattis. Keep aside and use as required.
7. If you want to cook these chapattis, just roast them for a little longer on both sides and serve hot with vegetable of your choice.

Nutritive values per chapatti

Energy	Protein	Carbohydrates	Fat	Fibre
69 cal	2.2 gm	12.5 gm	1.1 gm	0.3 gm

Total Health Series by Tarla Dalal

The Total Health series is a range of cookbooks specially designed and carefully researched by a team of qualified nutritionists. These books are an action-oriented guide for good health and wellness to suit the nutritional needs for different age groups, be it an expectant mum, a baby, an individual who has a medical problem or aims to lose weight. These books will help you and your family stay in fine fettle. They have opened new vistas in the field of cooking while providing you with healthy guidelines for adding verve and vitality to your life. Some of the titles in this series are:

Low Calorie Healthy Cooking   *Pregnancy Cook Book*   *Baby & Toddler Cook Book*   *Healthy Heart Cook Book*   *Cooking with 1 Teaspoon of Oil*   *Delicious Diabetic Recipes*